Innerseas by Ferdinand Jónsson
publication date 21 June 2025

Innerseas brings Ferdinand Jónsson's poetry to English readers for the first time, in poems that hymn wildness and wilderness, our human place in the landscape and the landscapes within our psyche.

'The book is simply beautiful... full of life and colour, but also contemplative... as it follows the migrating birds whose journeys we watch with all the longing for freedom that is in us.'
(Védís Skarphéðinsdóttir)

About the poet: Ferdinand Jónsson is from Kópavogur south of Reykjavik, and is the youngest son of a nurse and an artist. His family mostly originate from South Iceland, Eyrabakki, Stokkseyri and Flói, an area between the big rivers. He has published three poetry collections in Iceland with Veröld: *Innsævi* (2013), *Í úteyjum* (2016), and *Af djúpum straumi* (2022). He's lived in London for nearly thirty years, and works for the NHS as a Consultant Psychiatrist and Associate Clinical Director for Inpatient Services, in Tower Hamlets for the East London Foundation Trust. *Innerseas* is the first translation of his work into English.

About the publisher: Pottery Press books often explore connections between word and image; the word 'translated' into material form. *Innerseas* includes colour prints of Liz Mathews' artist's books setting some of the poems, with the words in both languages. The poems are also printed in Icelandic as well as English, exploring the resonances and reflections between the two ancient languages.

THE POTTERY PRESS

thepotterypress.wordpress.com/innerseas/

Innerseas

Ferdinand Jónsson

The Pottery Press

First published in London in 2025 by
The Pottery Press
Potters' Yard
London N19 5EX
www.pottersyard.co.uk
thepotterypress.wordpress.com

With thanks to Veröld, publishers of *Innsævi*, 2013

ISBN: 978-0-9930171-6-2

A CIP record for this book
is available from the British Library

Designed by The Pottery Press
Printed by Imprint Digital

Bókin er tileinkuð foreldrum mínum,
Helgu Óskarsdóttur
og Jóni Ferdinandssyni

This book is dedicated to my parents,
Helga Óskarsdóttir
& Jón Ferdinandsson

Translated with the poet from Icelandic into English
by Annie Turner, Kate Newmann and Joan Newmann

and revised with the poet for this edition
by Frances Bingham & Liz Mathews
for The Pottery Press

Together

come
into the quiet

think no more

in the dreamlike
veil
of the rainy
days

touch
thc palc facc
of spring

Fylgd

komdu
inn í kyrrðina

gleymdu

í draumkenndum
hjúp
hinna regnvotu
daga

fölan vanga
vorsins
snertu

Meðfram veginum hlaðna það er þarna
Along the stony lane there it is
further up the river
það er þarna
there it is
undir víðum himni nýjum
under a wide new sky
vorið
spring
gegnum hliðið
through the old gate
in the middle of the meadow

The meadow

there
it is

further up the river
along
the stony lane

there
it is

through
the old gate

in the middle
of the meadow
under a wide
new sky

spring

Engið

það er
þarna

inn með ánni
meðfram veginum
hlaðna

það er
þarna

gegnum hliðið
gamla

úti á enginu
undir víðum himni
nýjum

vorið

April

heavy
clouds
southern skies

a restless
refuge
early
spring

in a white-yellow
deserted land

whooper swans

at a frozen lake
their benevolent
ancestral
home

too early

April
most cruel
of months

Apríl

undir þungum
skýjum
suðurloftsins

í hvikulu
skjóli
vorsins
nýja

í gulhvítri
víðáttu

álftir

á frosnu vatni
óðalsins
gamla
gjöfula

en of snemma

apríl
harðastur
mánaða

Landsong	Landslag
in the distance	úr fjarlægð
mountains	rísa
rise	fjöll
clean	hin hreinu
forms	form
white	hvít
light	flæðir
streams	birta
clear	frá
lucent	tærum
blue	bláma
unknown	hins óþekkta
land	lands
within	innra

The secret

in the fog
in this floating
drizzle

among the angelica
an aroma
so heavy
so eager
the centre
of a dream
where a secret
sleeps

let
me
gently
touch
your face

Leyndarmál

í þokunni
í þessum syndandi
úða

á meðal hvanna
sem ilma
svo þungar
svo áfjáðar
mitt
í draumnum
þar sem leyndarmálið
sefur

leyf
mér
að snerta
andlit
þitt

Stars

there is sand
in the grass

a kettle
in the dark

I can hear
Night
her cold
breath

and maybe stars
late summer stars

if only you
were
here

Stjörnur

það er sandur
í grasinu

ketill
í myrkrinu

það heyrist
í nóttinni
hún andar
köldu

og kannski stjörnur
síðsumarstjörnur

ef þú
værir
hér

Kvöld

í uppábúnu rúmi
undir vetrarsængum
hvítum
í kvöldsins
þögn

heitur
kyrrlátur
söknuður

Evening

in a made-up bed
under white
winter
quilts
at the end
of the evening

gentle
wistful
yearning

Night

in the tender
night-rain
of the past
you will
arrive
once more

say
goodbye

Nótt

í mildu
næturregni
hins liðna
kemur
þú
aftur

til að
kveðja

In the garden

someone left them here
angels
in the night

the snowflakes danced
in the evening air
as if they were free

the snow keeps falling
snow filling my life
silent joy

I want to whisper
through this winter wall
reach your ears
speak truth
without words

and countless
flying angels
in the garden
in the night

Í garðinum

einhver skildi þá eftir
englana
í nótt

snjókornin dönsuðu
í kvöldloftinu
sem væru þau frjáls

það snjóar alltaf
fönnin fyllir líf mitt
hljóðlátum fögnuði

vil hvísla
gegnum kófið
ná eyrum þínum
segja sannleikann
án orða

og ótal
fljúgandi englar
í garðinum
í nótt

Lake Kleifarvatn	Við Kleifarvatn
leaden clouds	hin þungu ský
of early	vorsins
spring	unga
silently touch	snerta þögn
white	hraunsins
lava land	hvíta
winter hides	veturinn felur
my old	fjöllin
mountains	gömlu
in the wasteland	í auðninni
east wind	austanvindur
awakens the deep	vekur vatnið
old lake	djúpa
stroking	gamla
ancient	strengi
strings	strýkur
my anguish	angist mína
eases	hylur

Inland

beyond roads
hidden in fog
far heathlands
in green moss
at the spring
in the centre
alive
in clear water
a feeling
for you

Innlönd

utan vega
hulin þoku
lengst inni á heiðinni
í grænum mosa
við vatnaskil
allra átta
vakir
í tæru vatni
tilfinning
um þig

World

in washed
floors
cleaned
windowsills
in an old
mirror
time
expands
with
all
its heart

alone
indoors

Veröld

í skúruðum
gólfum
þvegnum
gluggakistum
í gömlum
spegli
teygist
tíminn
af
öllu
hjarta

innan
dyra

Time

in white
closed
cabinets

in pots
and pans
unloved

in locked
boxes
sacred

preserved
time

Tími

í hvítum
skápum
lokuðum

í pottum
pönnum
ósnertum

í læstum
hirslum
heilögum

óbreytt
tímatal

Sumar

blóm
á borði

blámi
í krukku

væntingar
í stofu

veðraskil

í dag
flýg ég
frjáls

Summer

tulips
on the table

blueness
in the jar

longing
in the living room

a change
in the weather

today
I fly
free

Morning

the abyss
of misfortune
is full
of black
boulders

in the stillness
at dawn
they align
themselves
in circles

the water turns again
blue
with hope

Morgunn

hylur
óhamingjunnar
er fullur
af steinum
svörtum

og í kyrrðinni
þá er dagur
rís
raðast þeir
í hringi

vatnið verður aftur
blátt
af óskum

Under the rowan

listen
with
your heart

in the air
autumn

the silent
song

soon
will come
the first
embrace
of winter

Undir reynitrjánum

hlustaðu
með
hjartanu

haustið
nálgast

hinn hljóði
söngur

senn
kemur
fyrsta
faðmlag
vetrar

Thingvellir	Þingvellir
night	nóttin
sleeps	sefur
in Nikulásargjá	í Nikulásargjá
lingberry	lynginu
bleeding	blæðir
blue and red	bláu og rauðu
the wind	vindurinn
claims	tekur
the leaves	laufið til sín
into eased	inn í kvíðalausa
stillness	kyrrð
winter arrives	kemur vetur

Illness I

in a ravine
between sky-high
mountains
where the blue
glaciers
soar
silence
resides
alone

the grip
the fear
in this freezing
river

don't
let go
though the torrent
strengthens
darkness
deepens

soon
morning
on the sand

in your palm
winged
hope

Veikindi I

í gljúfri
milli himinhárra
fjalla
þar sem bláir
jöklar
gnæfa
býr
þögnin
ein

hönd
og angist
í ískaldri
ánni

slepptu
ekki
þó strauminn
herði
þó myrkrið
dýpki

senn
morgnar
á sandi

í lófa
vængjuð
von

Illness II

this is too
long

in the unbearable
light
of uncertainty

this is too
long

few
will
notice
no one
will
utter
a word
unless
you
touch
the heavens

I
go
nowhere

Veikindi II

þetta er of
langt

í óbærilegu
ljósi
óvissunnar

þetta er of
langt

fáir
það
vita
enginn
mun
orð
mæla
nema
þú
snertir
himininn

ég
fer
hvergi

Sleep

sleeping
in the slow
breeze
beneath soft summer
shawls

in the sunshine
they swim
through my mind
images
that belong
in the dreams
of others

Svefn

sef
í hægum
svala
undir sumartjöldum
mjúkum

í sólinni
er sem syndi
um meðvitund
mína
myndir
úr annarra
draumum

Reiði

í briminu
drukkknuðu mávar

frá grösugri sveit
hvarf
sólin

úr sortanum
risu
fjöll

gengu yfir
góðan
vin

Rage

in the surf
seagulls drowned

from the green
pastures
the sun
disappeared

out of blackness
mountains
rose

they walked over
my beautiful
friend

# Madrid	# Madríd
the city	borg
of the night	næturinnar
is warmer	er heitari
tender	hreyfing
is the movement	mannanna
of men	mýkri
their gaze	augnaráð
deeper	dýpri
air	mettað
suffused	hunangi
with honey	loftið
standing	standa
in the dark	í myrkrinu
black	svartir
virile	griðungar
bulls of Spain	Spánar
young	ólga
blood	í blóði
surges	ungu
desperation	í óþreyju
waits	bíða
now	núna
love	er
belongs	ástin
to beasts	nautanna

On the mountain

white
bread

red
rivers

five
fish
silver

in light
unearthly
with
warm
eyes
the young
man's
lips
open

Á fjallinu

hvítt
brauð

rauður
vökvi

fimm
fiskar
silfraðir

í ljósi
óræðu
með
heitum
augum
opnast
varir
unga
mannsins

Lovers

dark images
of night
soaring

born
in the cold twilight
of unease

in the morning
haze
they softly leave
in a warm
silence

your
closeness

Elskendur

dimmar myndir
nætur
flugu

úr kvíðarökkri
komu
köldu

í morgunmistri
mýktust
burt
í hlýrri
þögn

nálægðar
þinnar

Innsævi

flæðir
um brjóstið
birta
hvít
undan hverfandi móðu
morguns

yfir fallnar vonir
vetrar
vorskip
á innsævi
augna
þinna

Innerseas

through my heart
white light
flows
within drifting
morning
mist

over fallen hopes
of winter
ship of spring
glimpsed
in the innerseas
of your eyes

August

seductive
shadows
of a night
long gone
young
breeze
fragrant
branches
a night song
is near
the smallest bird
is singing
hidden in
the clearing
of love

Ágúst

í skuggum
seiðandi
kvöldsins
liðna
þytur
ungur
ilmandi greina
náttsöngur
nálægur
fuglsins minnsta
hulinn
á engi
innileikans

Great Northern Diver	Himbrimi
on the blue	á djúpu
mountain's	vatni
deep lake	fjallsins
distant	bláa
song	fjarlægur
dark	söngur
mournful	dimmur
beauty	fagur
some summer	sumar
nights	nætur
silent	hljóðar
howling	lofar
praises	lífið
good life	góða
touches	snertir
the pure	landið
sacred	hreina
land	eina

# Great Auk I	# Geirfugl I
of all	allra
birds	fugla
most agile	fimastur
fishing	fiskar
in the sea	í hafi
green	grænu
cold	köldu
home is	heima
the hidden islets	á hulduskerjum
deep	djúpur
song	söngur
of summer	sumars
lost	öllum
in the waves	öldum
of sea-dusk	horfinn
centuries	í sæhúmið
Alka	*Alka*
Impennis	*Impennis*

Geirfugl II

álkubróðir
í sumarsænum
yfir árþúsundir
í djúpinu
flýgur
frjáls

á löngu
liðnu
sumri
Íslands
einn
með unga
á bakinu
í briminu
hljóður
hulinn
í öldu-
földum
fortíðar

fuglinn
sem fórst

Great Auk II

razorbill's brother
in summer seas
centuries
of deep
flying
free

distant
Icelandic
summer
alone
with fledgling
on its back
silent
in the surf
hidden
breaking
waves
have passed

the bird
we lost

At Svínanes

on white sand
sea bluebell
shows
the way
into a world
of forgotten dreams

in a clear sky
sea eagle

soft hillside mires
cliffs
home
to the hidden people

night falling

I travel afar
the trackless road
bound
by the wasteland beauty
of these fjords

Á Svínanesi

á hvítum sandi
vísa bláliljur
veg
inn í heim horfinna
drauma

í heiðríkju
haförn

hallamýrar
mjúkar
yfir hulduklettum

kvöldar

um vegleysu ferðast
burt
bundinn
eyðifegurð
fjarða

Photograph

two women
one older
dressed
in long
black
skirts

tired faces
longing
for a better life

maybe not
I know
nothing
about
them

apart from
safe-keeping
of old words
in my house
in my head

Ljósmynd

tvær konur
fátækar
önnur eldri
klæddar síðum
pilsum
svörtum

í þreyttum svip
von
um betri tíð

og þó
ég
veit
ekkert
um þær

nema
að þær gæta
gamalla orða
í húsi mínu
og huga

My family

when my family
have left
evening falls
in my soul
their faces
will
fade

if only
you
could
come
without
words
in your
eyes

Fólkið mitt

þegar fólkið mitt
er farið
og kvöldar
í sálinni
máist
mynd þess
burt

bara
ef þú gætir
komið
án
allra
orða
í augum
þínum

Earth

I keep
in the grass
close to the roots
under the larch tree
that belonged to my father
pure earth

in our
garden
in the breeze
from the south
I keep
the kind
summer

Jörð

geymi
í grasinu
við ræturnar
undir lerkitrénu
sem faðir minn átti
hreina jörð

í garði
okkar
í golu
af suðri
geymi
sumarið
góða

Farewell

rest
in the familiar
wind
under the aspen
fragrances
of summer

I know
you dwell
on the hill
where the mountains
mark
the sky
above clear colours
of autumn

wait for me
where the river
meets the sea
on the shore
that keeps
the memory
of our
land

Kveðja

hvíldu
í kunnuglegri
golunni
undir öspunum
þegar ilmar
af sumri

veit
þú hvílir
á hæðinni
þar sem fjöllin
marka
himininn
yfir tærum litum
haustsins

bíddu mín
þar sem fljótið
mætir hafinu
á ströndinni
sem geymir
minninguna
um landið
okkar

River Thjorsa

before
the redshank
awakens
while the grass
glitters
with dew
where the river
spreads wide
my heart
fills with
peace

north
fair
mountains
untouched
glaciers
July night
summer
scents
of Iceland

a blue dawn
deep in my mind
over all my days
and beyond
into
the morning

Á Þjórsárbökkum

áður en
stelkurinn
vaknar
meðan grasið
glitrar
af dögg
þar sem fljótið
breiðir úr sér
um hjartað
streymir
friður

fjöllin
tær
í norðri
ósnertir
jöklar
júlínætur
angan
af sumri
Íslands

dagrenning blá
úr djúpi hugans
yfir daga mína
yfir dauðann
inn
í morguninn

Summerland

the snipe
thrumming
in the night
time
slowly passing
red-throated diver
awake
shallow water
green
dark

reed-beds dreaming
sleeping celandine
in the land of summer
night

sedge-grass lives
the greylag goose
protects

an eagle glides

alone

Sumarland

gaukur í kvöldinu
tifar
tíminn hægur
líður
lómur vakir
á grunnu vatni
grænu
dimmu

stararflóð dreymir
er sólir sofa
í sumarlandi
nætur

fífusund lifir
gæsamóðir
gætir

flýgur örn yfir

einn

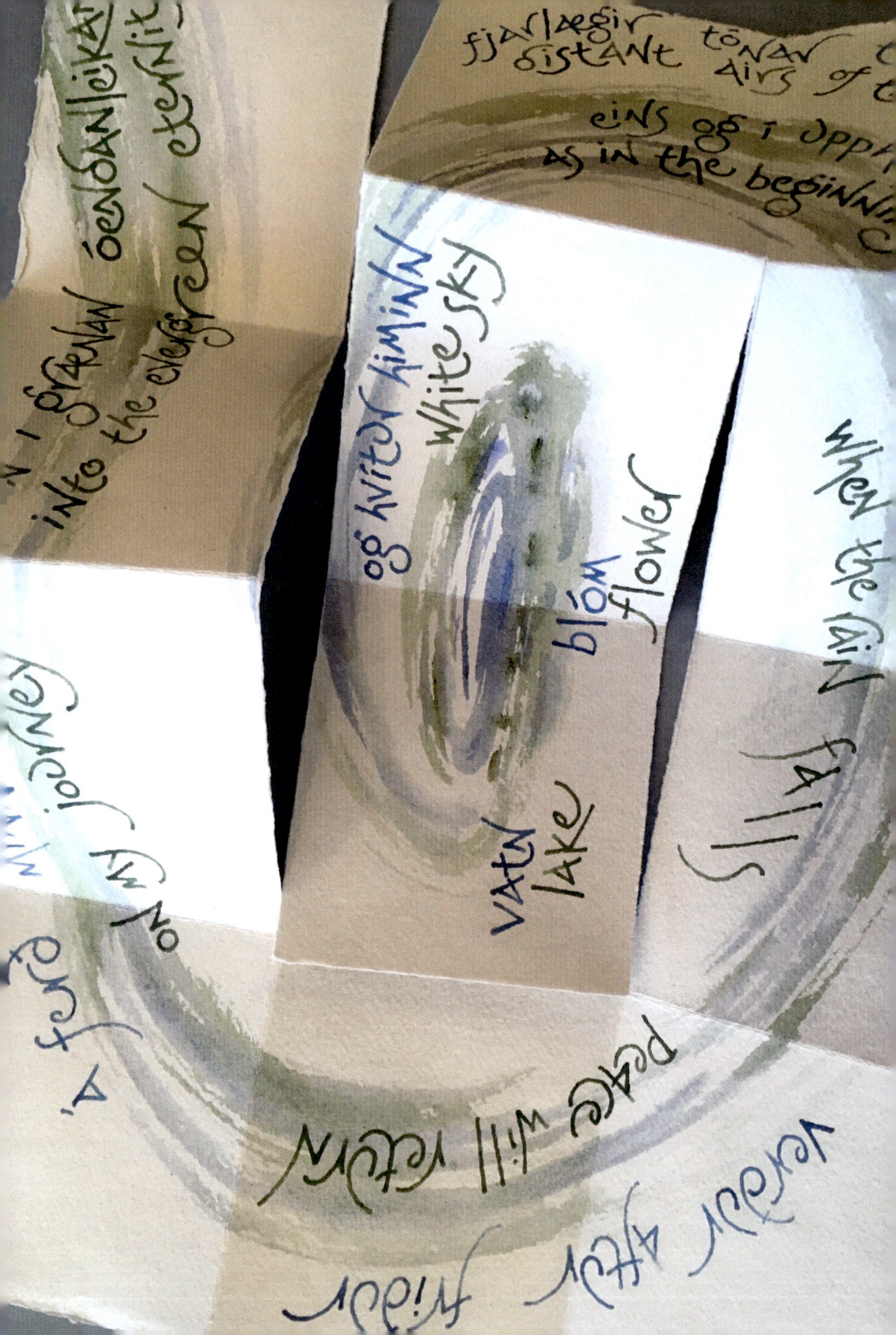

fjarlægir tónar
distant airs of
eins og í upph
as in the beginni
í grænan óendanleikan
into the evergreen eternit
og hvítur himinn
white sky
blóm
flower
vatn
lake
when the rain falls
á ferð
on my journey
peace will return
friður verður aftur

Journey

lake
flower
white sky

distant
airs
of the wooden flute
as in the beginning

when the rain
falls
peace
will return

on my journey
into
the evergreen
eternity

Ferðalag

vatn
blóm
og hvítur himinn

fjarlægir
tónar
tréflautunnar
eins og í upphafi

þegar regnið
fellur
verður aftur
friður

á ferð
minni
inn í grænan
óendanleikann

List of poems

Notes for the English translation

Innerseas, title and poem on p26: the word *innsævi* carries both the meaning of the sea closest to the land and the sea within you.

Landsong, p5: *Landslag,* literally landscape, can also mean the song of the land.

late summer stars, p7: *síðsumarstjörnur* is a new coinage in Icelandic, a language which allows the creation of new composite words. Also **sea-dusk**, p29: *sæhúmið.*

Thingvellir, p18: *Þingvellir,* original meeting-place of Iceland's parliament, Althing, the great-grandmother of all parliaments; a landscape of great significance and a 'national shrine'.

Nikulásargjá, p18: Nikulás gorge, a deep fissure within Thingvellir National Park filled with clear blue water which darkens as it deepens, as though night is sleeping down there during the day.

Great Northern Diver, p28: *Himbrimi,* a large bird, strikingly patterned in black and white, of the specialised ancient family of divers: streamlined, long-necked, fish-catching birds. During dusk and at night they call with a beautiful, unearthly sound.

some summer nights, p28: *sumar* means both some and summer in Icelandic; in the same poem *hljóðar* can mean silent and also howling. On p29 the word *öldum* can translate as waves or centuries, or both.

Great Auk, p29: *Geirfugl,* huge flightless sea-bird from the auk family, hunted to extinction in Iceland. Now much mourned in silence, possibly with some shame, as Icelanders killed the last remaining pair on 3rd June 1844. However Icelanders were a very poor population, constantly on the verge of starvation, and were paid by Danish and English aristocrats and foreign museums to get the last remaining birds. In addition volcanic activities submerged the last islets where the birds were safe. Quite possibly the shame belongs to all of us? But most importantly, if we own this, the power of the mourning and shame for this majestic bird could be a blessing for us all.

the hidden people, p31: *hulduklettum,* mythic nature-spirits of Iceland, the invisible Icelandic population, still deeply respected, and through the generations bringing a sense of security and fellowship in a harsh Icelandic environment; inspiration for Tolkien's noble elven race. As well as these cliffs, **the hidden islets**, p29, *á hulduskerjum,* also belong to the hidden people.

About the poet

Ferdinand Jónsson is from Kópavogur south of Reykjavik, and is the youngest son of a nurse and an artist. His family mostly originate from South Iceland, Eyrabakki, Stokkseyri and Flói, an area between the big rivers. He has published three poetry collections in Iceland with Veröld: *Innsævi* (2013), *Í úteyjum* (2016), and *Af djúpum straumi* (2022). He's lived in London for nearly thirty years, and works for the NHS as a Consultant Psychiatrist and Associate Clinical Director for Inpatient Services in Tower Hamlets, for the East London Foundation Trust.

Innerseas is the first translation of his poetry into English.

Images

Meadow, p2: artist's book by Liz Mathews,
watercolour on handmade paper 42 x 30cm.

Journey, p38 and cover: artist's book by Liz Mathews,
watercolour on handmade paper 42 x 30cm.

Acknowledgements

Grateful thanks to Veröld, the Icelandic publishers of *Innsævi.*

Also to Valgerður Benediktsdóttir,
Annie Turner, Kate Newmann and Joan Newmann,
Frances Bingham & Liz Mathews.

Innerseas
by Ferdinand Jónsson

is a Pottery Press Poetry Publication

Other Pottery Press publications include:

MOTHERTONGUE
Frances Bingham & Liz Mathews

Paper Wings
Poems by Maureen Duffy, set to paper by Liz Mathews

Past Present: Piers Plowless & Sir Orfeo
Maureen Duffy

The Blue Hour of Natalie Barney
Frances Bingham

Under the Quarry Woods
Jeremy Hooker

London Panopticon
Frances Bingham, with images by Liz Mathews

Wanderer
Maureen Duffy

THE POTTERY PRESS

www.pottersyard.co.uk
thepotterypress.wordpress.com